Having Fun with the
for Children 5 & Up.

How the Book & Videos Work

The Book

As a music professor and guitar teacher for over twenty five years, I have wanted to help young, beginner guitar students succeed in playing famous and beautiful music. In the past, beginner guitar books for children have taken a dull and uninspiring approach. Most of the time these books just throw together songs and techniques in a random, boring, and confusing way; sometimes these books are no better than blurry photocopies.

This book and video course takes a new and innovative approach!

Guitar Book for Kids 5 & Up makes learning famous guitar songs fun, easy, interactive, and engaging. The book and streaming videos follow a step-by-step lesson format for learning some of the most famous music and playing these songs for family and friends!

In *Guitar Book for Kids 5 & Up,* each lesson builds on the previous one in a clear and easy-to-understand manner. No music reading is necessary. I walk the child through how to play these wonderful songs, starting with very easy music, at the beginning of the book, and advancing, little by little, as they master new repertoire and techniques. As your child is able to play these new songs, he or she will also greatly improve on the guitar! Along the way, there are even some jokes to make learning fun.

If you have always wanted your child to play the guitar, then, this book is for you. Let's get started on this exciting musical journey!

The Videos

There are Free, Streaming Video Lessons that coincide with the material presented in *Guitar Book for Kids 5 & Up.* The lesson videos cover playing songs and pieces, guitar technique, tuning, the parts of the guitar, basic music elements and fundamentals, and how to develop good practice habits. All of these videos are free. To access the videos, go to SteeplechaseMusic.com and click on the link for Guitar Books at top of the Home Page. Then, on the Guitar Books Page, click on the cover image for the *Guitar Book for Kids 5 & Up.* On the webpage for the *Guitar Book for Kids 5 & Up,* you will see a link / image for the video lessons. Click on the link / image for access.

Here is a list of some of the <u>Great</u> <u>Guitar</u> Music that you will learn in this book:

- *Ode to Joy* by Beethoven
- *Happy Birthday*
- *Amazing Grace*
- *Take Me Out to the Ballgame*
- *Jingle Bells*
- *Kum-Bah-Yah*
- *Silent Night*
- *Yankee Doodle*
- *Old MacDonald*
- *Shenandoah*
- *When the Saints Go Marching In*
- *Mary Had a Little Lamb*
- *Brahms' Famous Lullaby*
- *This Little Light of Mine*
- *The Alphabet Song*
- *Simple Gifts*
- *Home on the Range*
- *Hickory Dickory Dock*
- *The Farmer in the Dell*
- *Skip to My Lou*
- *The Muffin Man*
- And Many More Songs and Pieces!

You will also learn how to read music, play chords, as well as many more exciting guitar techniques!

T a bl of C u nt nts

Page:

Table of Contents for the Video Lessons

Important!

To access the video lessons, go to steeplechasemusic.com and click on the link at the top of the page for Guitar Books. Then, from the Guitar Books webpage, click on the image for this book, "Guitar Book for Kids 5 & Up". On the webpage for the *Guitar Book for Kids 5 & Up*, you will see a link to Video Lessons. Click that link for the Video Lessons webpage for this book. The video lessons are free and there is no limit on the number of times you may watch them.

Guitar Book for Kids 5 & Up - Beginner Lessons : Learn to Play
Famous Guitar Songs for Children, How to Read Music & Guitar
Chords (Book & Streaming Videos)

by Damon Ferrante

For additional information about
music books, recordings, and concerts, please visit the Steeplechase
website: www.steeplechasearts.com

Steeplechase Music Instruction

Also by Damon Ferrante

Piano Book for Kids 5 & Up

Beginner Rock Guitar Lessons

Piano Book for Adult Beginners

Guitar Book for Adult Beginners

Guitar Scales Handbook

Beginner Classical Piano Music

Piano Scales, Chords & Arpeggios Lessons

Getting Started & Having Fun

Parts of the Guitar

Here is a Diagram of a Guitar.

Try to find these parts on your guitar. If you have an electric guitar, it might look a little bit different. **Have Fun!**

See Video 1

This is the head of the guitar.

This is a fret.

This is a string.

This is the neck of the guitar.

This is the sound hole.

This is the pickguard.

This is the bridge.

This is the body of the guitar.

You can find the video lesson at steeplechasemusic.com

Nam s of the St. ings

In this lesson, we are going to learn about the letter names for the guitar strings.

See Video 2

Low					High
E	A	D	G	B	E

The Guitar Strings

- 6th String, **Low E = Every**
- 5th String, **A = Alligator**
- 4th String, **D = Drinks**
- 3rd String, **G = Grape Juice**
- 2nd String, **B = Before**
- 1st String, **High E = Eating**

- The guitar has six strings.
- The strings have numbers that go from the thinnest string to the thickest string.
- The thinnest string is string #1. It is located closest to the floor and it has the highest sound.
- The thickest string is string #6. It is located closest to the ceiling and has the lowest (or deepest) sound.
- The thinnest string (the first string) is called the "High E String".
- The thickest string (the sixth string) is called the "Low E String".

- Going from thickest string to thinnest string, here are the letter names for the strings:
  Low E, A, D, G, B, High E.
- To help you remember the letter names and order for the strings, here is a funny sentence: **E**very **A**lligator **D**rinks **G**rape Juice **B**efore **E**ating.
- The first letter of each word (**except for "juice"**) stands for a string of the guitar, going from thickest string to thinnest string. **See the chart on the left.**

Holding the Guitar

First, let's find a comfortable chair or couch and sit down with the guitar.

To hold the guitar, put the guitar on your right leg, in your lap. Then, place your right hand over the front of the guitar body, so that your hand is in front of the sound hole. Bring your left hand under the guitar neck and gently place your fingers over the strings.

Now, you're ready to make some great music and have fun!

Try Playing the open Strings for this song.
The E String is <u>Underlined</u>. The B String is in *Italics*.

At the Starting Line

<u>E</u> <u>E</u> *B* *B* | <u>E</u> <u>E</u> <u>E</u> <u>E</u> | <u>E</u> <u>E</u> *B* *B* | <u>E</u> <u>E</u> <u>E</u> <u>E</u>

12

Holding the Guitar Pick

See Video 3

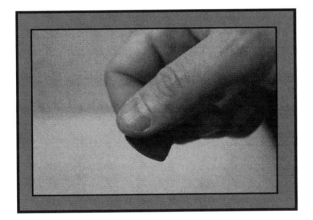

Let's now look at how to hold the guitar pick.

- Gently place the guitar pick on the finger nail of your Right-Hand Index Finger.
- It should be resting gently on top of your finger nail.
- Then, slide it to the left side of your Index Finger.
- Finally, gently place your Right-Hand Thumb over over the guitar pick. It should be held between your Right-Hand Thumb and Index Finger.

Try Playing the open Strings for this song.
The E String is <u>Underlined</u>.
The B String is in *Italics*.

Race Cars

<u>E</u> <u>E</u> *B B* | <u>E</u> <u>E</u> <u>E</u> <u>E</u> | *B B* <u>E</u> <u>E</u> | *B* <u>E</u> <u>E</u> <u>E</u>

Joke Time! "Knock, Knock." "Who's There?" "Lettuce"." "Lettuce, who?" "Let us in; it's lunchtime." Ha! Ha! Ha!

13

Left-Hand Position

Now, let's learn about how to use the left hand when we play the guitar. It's important to always play on the tips of our left-hand fingers, when we press down a string to make a note on the guitar. If we don't use the tips of our left-hand fingers, we may miss the note, play an "extra / wrong" note, or make the string buzz. **Check Out Video 4 to see this technique.**

Try Playing the open Strings for this song.
The E String is <u>Underlined</u>. The B String is in *Italics*.
The 3rd String (the G String) is **Bold**.

See Video 4

Mountain Sunrise

<u>E</u> <u>E</u> *B B* | **G G G G** | *B B B B* | <u>E</u> <u>E</u> <u>E</u> <u>E</u> ‖

Notes on the 1st String

Let's learn 3 Notes on the 1st String.
E is the Open String: No Left Hand Needed.
F is on the 1st Fret. Use your Index Finger.
G is on the 3rd Fret. Use your Ring Finger.

See Video 5

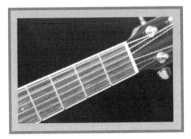

F

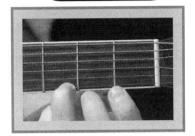

G

The Open **E** 1st String

1st Fret of the
1st String

3rd Fret of the
1st String

Try this song that uses 3 notes on the 1st String.
E is <u>underlined</u>. F is in *italics*. G is **bold**. Have Fun!

Fun Balloons

| <u>E</u> <u>E</u> **G** **G** | <u>E</u> <u>E</u> <u>E</u> <u>E</u> | <u>E</u> <u>E</u> *F* *F* | <u>E</u> <u>E</u> <u>E</u> |

Joke Time! "What did the Teddy Bear say after dinner?"
"No dessert for me; I'm stuffed." Ha! Ha! Ha!

15

Songs on the 1st String

Try this song that uses 3 notes on the 1st String.
E is <u>underlined</u>. F is in *italics*. G is **bold**. Have Fun!

Jogging Puppy

See Video 6

| **G** **G** **G** <u>E</u> | *F* *F* *F* <u>E</u> | **G** <u>E</u> *F* <u>E</u> |

Check Out Video Lesson 6 for help tuning the guitar

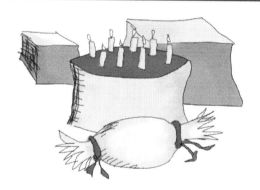

Birthday Fun

| <u>E</u> **G** <u>E</u> **G** | *F* **G** *F* **G** | **G** *F* <u>E</u> <u>E</u> | *F* <u>E</u> <u>E</u> <u>E</u> |

Joke Time! "What space villain works at a restaurant?"
"Darth Waiter!" Ha! Ha! Ha!

Counting & Measure.

- Music is composed of groups of beats called measures.
- Measures are set off by vertical lines, called bar lines.
- Measures most commonly contain 2, 3, or 4 beats.
- Below, are examples of sets of four measures in 4/4 time.
- In 4/4 time, you will count 4 beats for each measure.
  In other words, you will count: 1234, 1234, 1234, 1234.
- Try counting aloud and clapping the beats for the exercise below.

Example 1:

| 1 2 3 4 | 1 2 3 4 | 1 2 3 4 | 1 2 3 4 ‖

Example 2:
Try Clapping on the X: On the First Beat.

| 1 2 3 4 | 1 2 3 4 | 1 2 3 4 | 1 2 3 4 ‖
| X | X | X | X

Example 3:
Try Clapping on the X: On the First and Third Beats.

| 1 2 3 4 | 1 2 3 4 | 1 2 3 4 | 1 2 3 4 ‖
| X   X | X   X | X   X | X   X

Example 4:
Try Clapping on the X: On the Second Beat.

| 1 2 3 4 | 1 2 3 4 | 1 2 3 4 | 1 2 3 4 ‖
| X | X | X | X

Notes on the 2nd String

See Video 7

Let's learn 3 Notes on the 2nd String.
B is the Open String: No Left Hand Needed.
C is on the 1st Fret. Use your Index Finger.
D is on the 3rd Fret. Use your Ring Finger.

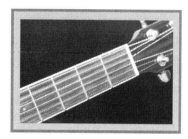  

B

The Open 2nd String

C

1st Fret of the
2nd String

D

3rd Fret of the
2nd String

Try this song that uses 3 notes on the 2nd String.
B is <u>underlined</u>. C is in *italics*. D is **bold**. Have Fun!

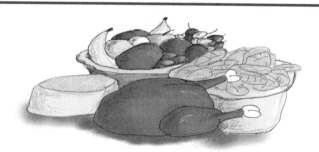

Thanksgiving Dinner

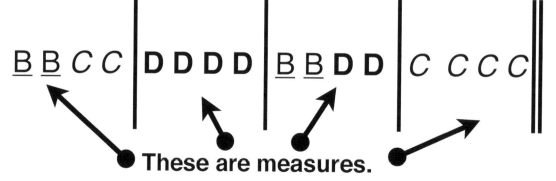

<u>B</u> <u>B</u> *C C* | **D D D D** | <u>B</u> <u>B</u> **D D** | *C C C C* ‖

These are measures.

18

Songs on 2nd String

> Try these songs that use **3 Notes** on the **2nd String**. The notes are **B, C, and D**. **Have Fun!**

Bouncing Ball

| C C B B | D D D D | C C B B | C C C C |

Rocket Ship

| C C C C | D D D D | B B B B | C C C C |

19

Tim Signatur s

- Measures are composed of groups of beats called Time Signatures or Meter (both terms mean the same thing and are interchangeable).
- The most common Time Signatures (or "meters") are groups of 2, 3, or 4 beats per measure: 2/4, 3/4, and 4/4 Time Signatures.
- 2/4 Time Signature groups the notes into measures of 2 beats. Count: "One, Two" for each measure.
- 3/4 Time Signature groups the notes into measures of 3 beats. Count: "One, Two, Three" for each measure.
- 4/4 Time Signature groups the notes into measures of 4 beats. Count: "One, Two, Three, Four" for each measure.
- Below, are examples of sets of four measures in 2/4, 3/4, and 4/4.
- Count aloud and clap on the first beat for the exercises below.

Example 1: 2/4 Time Signature
Try Clapping on the **X**: On the First Beat.

$\frac{2}{4}$
| 1   2 | 1   2 | 1   2 | 1   2 |
| X | X | X | X |

Example 2: 3/4 Time Signature
Try Clapping on the X: On the First Beat.

$\frac{3}{4}$
| 1   2   3 | 1   2   3 | 1   2   3 | 1   2   3 |
| X | X | X | X |

Example 3: 4/4 Time Signature
Try Clapping on the X: On the First Beat.

$\frac{4}{4}$
| 1   2   3   4 | 1   2   3   4 | 1   2   3   4 | 1   2   3   4 |
| X | X | X | X |

Try these songs that use **3 Notes** on the **1st and 2nd Strings**.
Here are the notes: B, C, D, E, F, G

Have Fun!

Mary's Little Lamb

4/4	E D C D	E E E	D D D	E G G
	Ma-ry had a	lit- tle lamb	lit- tle lamb	lit- tle lamb

Here is the Time Signature

E D C D	E E E E D	D E D	C
Ma-ry had a	lit- tle lamb its	fleece was white as	snow

Skip to My Lou

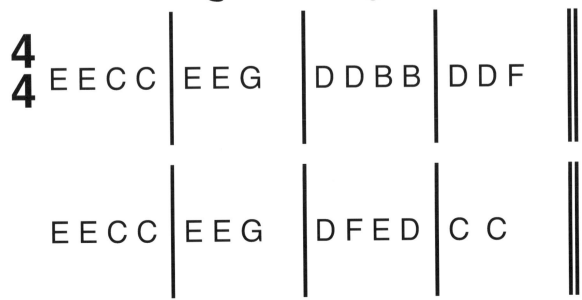

4/4	E E C C	E E G	D D B B	D D F

E E C C	E E G	D F E D	C C

21

Songs on 1st & 2nd Strings

Try these songs that use **3 Notes** on the **1st and 2nd Strings**.
Here are the notes: B, C, D, E, F, G

Have Fun!

Ode to Joy

$\frac{4}{4}$ | E E F G | G F E D | C C D E | E D D |

| E E F G | G F E D | C C D E | D C C ‖

Jingle Bells

$\frac{4}{4}$ | E E E | E E E | E G C D | E |
Jin-gle Bells, | Jin-gle Bels | Jin-gle all the | way. |

| F F F F | F E E E | E D D E | D G ‖
Oh, what fun it | is to ride on a | one horse open | sleigh. Hey!

22

Your Own Song

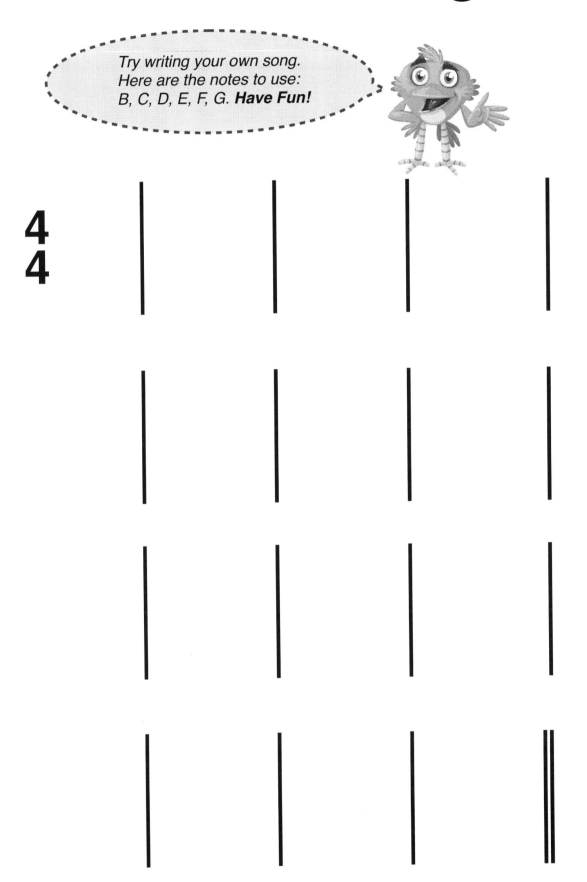

Try writing your own song.
Here are the notes to use:
B, C, D, E, F, G. **Have Fun!**

Whole Notes, Half Notes, and Quarter Notes

- Let's take a look at some basic rhythms.
- Quarter Notes are notes that get 1 Beat (or Count).
- Half Notes are notes that get 2 Beats (or Counts).
- Whole Notes are notes that get 4 Beats (or Counts).
- In the next 3 examples, try counting on each beat of the 4/4 measures aloud, for example: 1,2,3,4.
- Clap on the quarter, half, and whole notes.

♩ = 1 Beat   ♩ = 2 Beats   o = 4 Beats

Example 1:
Try Clapping on each "X", while counting the beats.

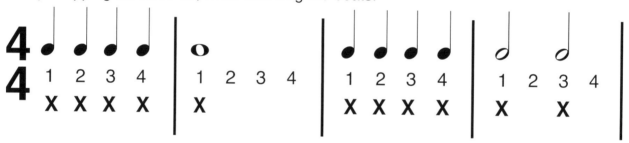

Example 2:
Try Clapping on each "X", while counting the beats.

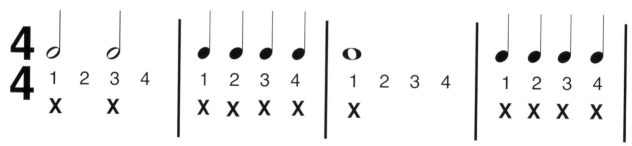

Example 3:
Try Clapping on each "X", while counting the beats.

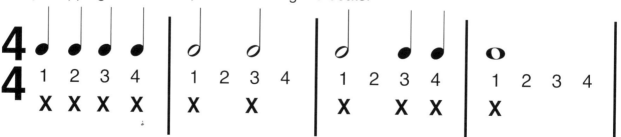

Whole Notes & Half Notes

> Try these songs that use **3 Notes** on the **1st String: E, F, and G.**
>
> **Have Fun!**

O   Whole Note = 4 Beats

♩   Half Note = 2 Beats

For Whole Notes Count: 1, 2, 3, 4
For Half Notes Count: 1, 2

The Happy Cat

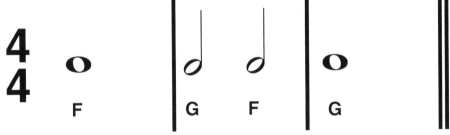

4/4	O		♩	♩		O	
	F		G	F		G	

Beats: 1 2 3 4   1 2 3 4   1 2 3 4

Raindrops

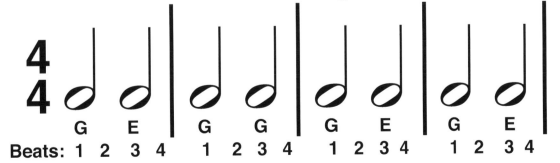

4/4	♩	♩	♩	♩	♩	♩	♩	♩
	G	E	G	G	G	E	G	E

Beats: 1 2 3 4   1 2 3 4   1 2 3 4   1 2 3 4

More Songs with Whole & Half Notes

Try these songs that use **3 Notes** on the **1st and 2nd Strings**.
B, C, D, E, F, and G.

Have Fun!

Sailboats

E F E   G F E

Beats: 1 2 3 4   1 2 3 4   1 2 3 4   1 2 3 4

Sunny Day

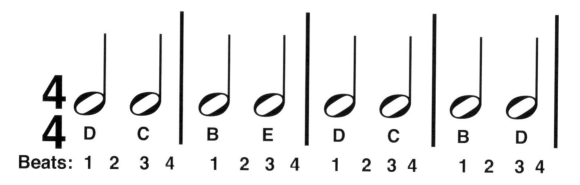

D C   B E   D C   B D

Beats: 1 2 3 4   1 2 3 4   1 2 3 4   1 2 3 4

Songs with Quarter Notes & Half Notes

Try these songs that use **3 Notes** on the **1st and 2nd Strings**: **B, C, D, E, F, and G.**

Have Fun!

Moonlight

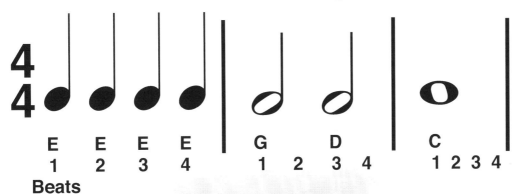

E E E E   G   D   C
1 2 3 4   1 2 3 4   1 2 3 4
Beats

Sleepy Chair

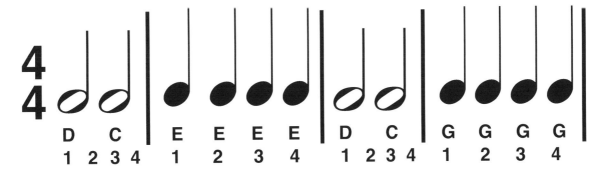

D C   E E E E   D C   G G G G
1 2 3 4   1 2 3 4   1 2 3 4   1 2 3 4

27

Songs with Quarter Notes, Half Notes & Whole Notes

Try these songs that use *3 Notes* on the *1st and 2nd Strings:*
B, C, D, E, F, and G.

Have Fun!

Summer Day

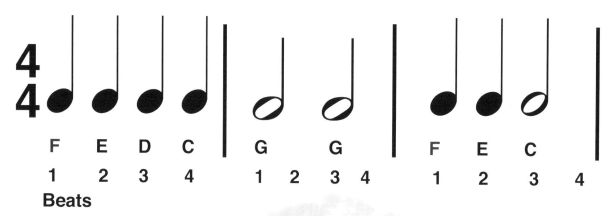

F	E	D	C	G	G	F	E	C
1	2	3	4	1 2 3 4		1	2	3 4

Beats

Bells Ringing

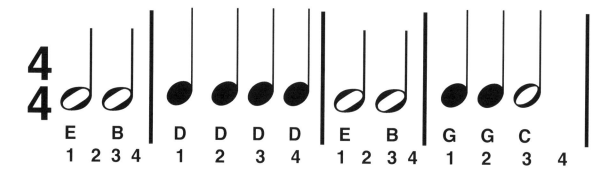

E	B	D	D	D	D	E	B	G	G	C
1 2 3 4		1	2	3	4	1 2 3 4		1	2	3 4

Notes on the 3rd String

Let's learn 2 Notes on the 3rd String.
G is the Open String: No Left Hand Needed.
A is on the 2nd Fret. Use your Middle Finger.

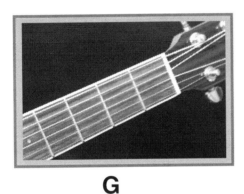

G

The Open 3rd String

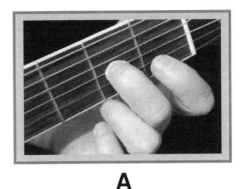

A

2nd Fret of the
3rd String

Happy Letters

29

Songs on the 3rd String

Let's learn two songs that use notes from the 3rd String: G and A.

Ice Cream Time

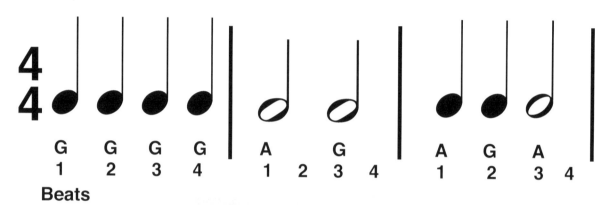

G	G	G	G	A	G	A	G	A
1	2	3	4	1	2 3 4	1	2	3 4

Beats

Clouds

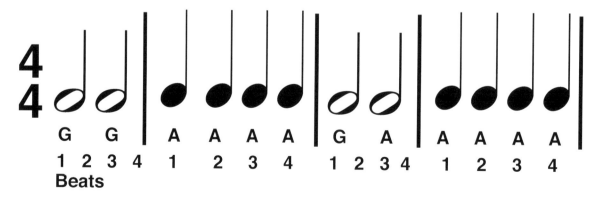

G	G	A	A	A	A	G	A	A	A	A	A
1 2	3 4	1	2	3	4	1 2	3 4	1	2	3	4

Beats

Let's try two new songs that use 2 and 3 strings.
In "Yankee Doodle", the **Underlined G** and the **Underlined A** are on the 3rd String (the G String). *Have Fun!*

Old MacDonald

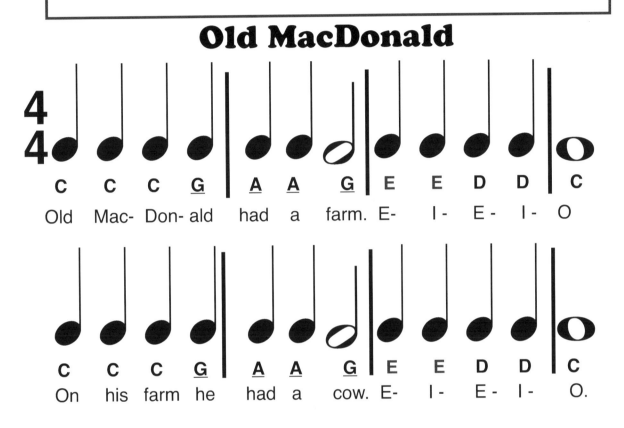

C	C	C	G	A	A	G	E	E	D	D	C
Old	Mac-	Don-	ald	had	a	farm.	E-	I-	E-	I-	O

C	C	C	G	A	A	G	E	E	D	D	C
On	his	farm	he	had	a	cow.	E-	I-	E-	I-	O.

Yankee Doodle

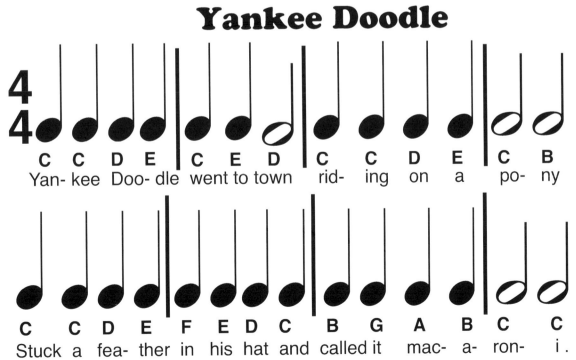

C	C	D	E	C	E	D	C	C	D	E	C	B
Yan-	kee	Doo-	dle	went	to	town	rid-	ing	on	a	po-	ny

C	C	D	E	F	E	D	C	B	G	A	B	C	C
Stuck	a	fea-	ther	in	his	hat	and	called	it	mac-	a-	ron-	i.

Try this song that is on strings 1, 2, and 3: the High E String, the B String, and the G String. The **Underlined "G"** and the **Underlined "A"** are on the 3rd String.

Remember to Count the Beats.

Have Fun!

Michael, Row the Boat Ashore

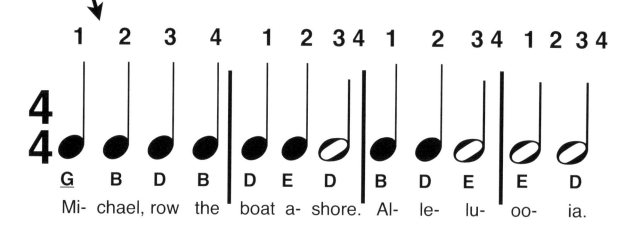

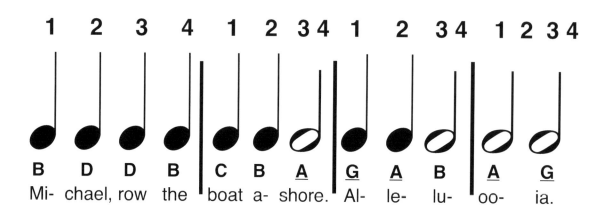

Notes on the 4th String

See Video 9

Let's learn 3 Notes on the 4th String.
D is the Open String: No Left Hand Needed.
E is on the 2nd Fret. Use your Index Finger.
F is on the 3rd Fret. Use your Middle Finger.

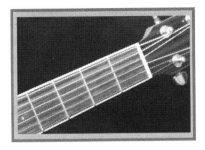

D
The Open 4th String

E
2nd Fret of the
4th String

F
3rd Fret of the
4th String

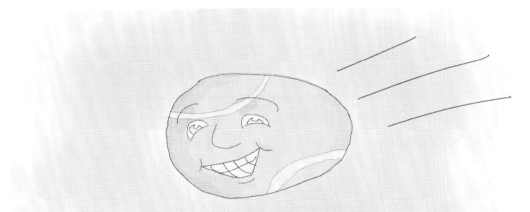

Tennis Fun

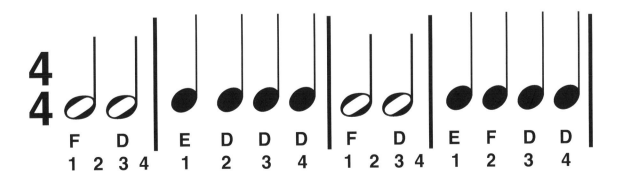

4/4	F	D	E	D	D	D	F	D	E	F	D	D
	1	2	3	4	1	2	3	4	1	2	3	4	1	2	3	4

A Song on the D String

Try this song that uses
3 Notes on the **4th String: D, E, and F.**
Have Fun!

Beats

Surfing the Waves

Songs on 3 & 4 Strings

Try these songs that use 3 & 4 Strings.
The **Underlined** "G" and "A" are on the 3rd String.

Twinkle, Twinkle, Little Star

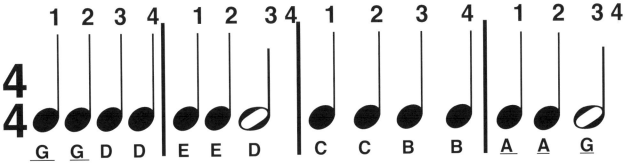

1	2	3	4	1	2	3 4	1	2	3	4	1	2	3 4
G	G	D	D	E	E	D	C	C	B	B	A	A	G

Twin-kle, Twin-kle, lit- tle star, how I won- der what you are.

We have a new kind of note: The Dotted Half Note.
It is equal to 3 Beats (or Counts)
Can you point to some Dotted Half Notes in *At the Ballpark?*

At the Ballpark

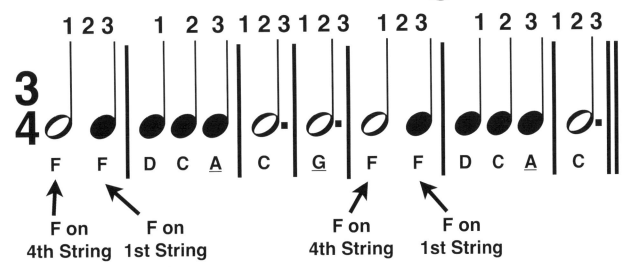

1 2 3	1	2	3 1 2 3 1 2 3	1 2 3	1 2 3 1 2 3
F	F	D C A C	G F	F D C A C

F on
4th String

F on
1st String

F on
4th String

F on
1st String

35

Strumming Chords

In this lesson, we are going to begin learning about playing chords.
Chords are groups of 3 or more notes that are played at the same time.
In the next few pages, we are going to start learning songs with chords.
Feel free to sing along at you strum the guitar. Also, a little later in the book
we are going to learn songs, where you can play the chords or the melody
Take some time to look over the chord symbols on this page. *Have Fun!*

Left-Hand Symbols:

1 • 1st Finger (Index Finger)

2 • 2nd Finger (Middle Finger)

3 • 3rd Finger (Ring Finger)

4 • 4th Finger (Pinky Finger)

O • Open String
(Let the String Vibrate.)

X • Mute String
(Block the String
with a Finger.)

• Place Finger
over 2 or more
strings.

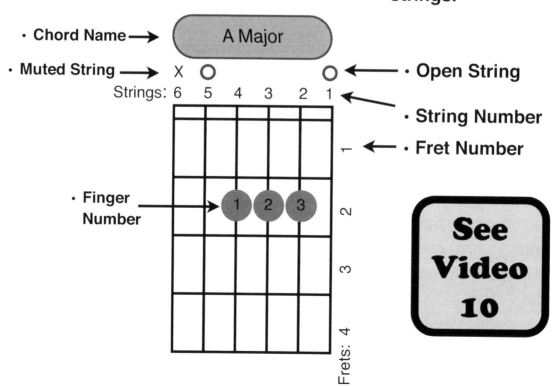

• Chord Name → A Major

• Muted String → X O ... O ← • Open String

Strings: 6 5 4 3 2 1 ← • String Number

← • Fret Number

• Finger Number → 1 2 3

See Video 10

The C Major Chord & G Major Chord

In this lesson, we are going to learn two new chords: C Major and G Major (see the diagrams). Remember to place the tips of your left-hand fingers on the strings when you play chords. Try playing 4 down-strums for each Measure.

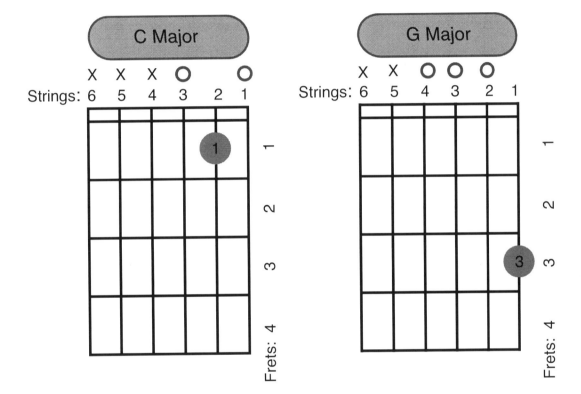

Rock & Roll Time!

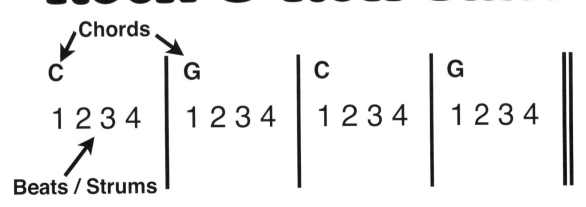

Chords

Beats / Strums

C   G   C   G

1 2 3 4   1 2 3 4   1 2 3 4   1 2 3 4

37

The F Major Chord

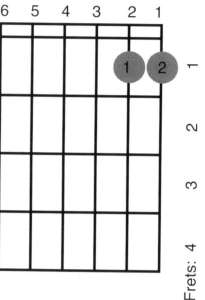

F Major

X X X X
Strings: 6 5 4 3 2 1

Frets: 4

Let's look at a new chord: F Major.
It uses only 2 strings: the 1st & 2nd.

In *Peace Like a River,* we have
three chords: C, F, and G.

Begin strumming on the second full
measure (during the word "peace").

Have Fun!

Peace Like a River

Chord:	(No Chord)		C		C		F	
		I've got	peace like a		river. I've got		Peace like a	
Strum:	1 2 3 4		1 2 3 4		1 2 3 4		1 2 3 4	

Chord:	C		C		C		G	
	river.	I've got	peace like a	river	in my	soul.		
Strum:	1 2 3 4		1 2 3 4		1 2 3 4		1 2 3 4	

Chord:	G		C		C		F	
		I've got	Peace like a		river. I've got		peace like a	
Strum:	1 2 3 4		1 2 3 4		1 2 3 4		1 2 3 4	

Chord:	C		C		G		C	
	river.	I've got	peace like a	river	in my	soul.		
Strum:	1 2 3 4		1 2 3 4		1 2 3 4		1 2 3 4	

Amazing Grace

> *Amazing Grace,* has three beats in each measure.
> Strum the chords three times per measure.
> If you have a question about how to play a chord,
> look back at the charts on the previous few pages.

Amazing Grace

Measure Line

Chord:	C	C	F	C
	A-mazing	Grace how	sweet the	sound that
Strum:	1 2 3	1 2 3	1 2 3	1 2 3

Chord:	C	C	G	G
	saved a	wretch like	me.	I
Strum:	1 2 3	1 2 3	1 2 3	1 2 3

Chord:	C	C	F	C
	once was	lost but	now am	found. Was
Strum:	1 2 3	1 2 3	1 2 3	1 2 3

Chord:	C	G	C	C
	blind but	now I	see.	
Strum:	1 2 3	1 2 3	1 2 3	1 2 3

Th C7 Cho. d

Let's look at the C7 chord.

It is played on three strings.

Make sure that you avoid playing the 4th, 5th, & 6th strings, when you are playing the C7 chord.

Can you find the C7 chord in *When the Saints*?

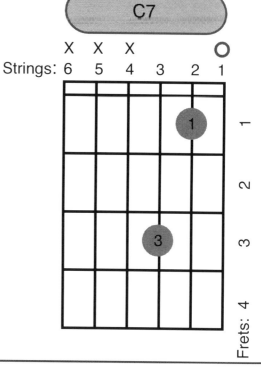

When the Saints

Chord:	(No Chord)	C	C	C
	Oh When the	Saints	go marchin' in	
Strum:	1 2 3 4	1 2 3 4	1 2 3 4	1 2 3 4
Chord: C		C	C7	G
	Oh When the	Saints go	marchin'	in
Strum:	1 2 3 4	1 2 3 4	1 2 3 4	1 2 3 4
Chord: G		C	C7	F
	Oh Lord, I	want to	be in that	number
Strum:	1 2 3 4	1 2 3 4	1 2 3 4	1 2 3 4
Chord: F		C	G	C
	Oh When the	Saints go	marchin'	in
Strum:	1 2 3 4	1 2 3 4	1 2 3 4	1 2 3 4

Reading

In the next section of this book, we are going to learn how to read music. It's a lot of fun! Plus, by learning how to read music, you are going to become a fantastic guitarist!

Great job so far!

The Treble Clef Lines: Overview

- Now, we are going to learn a little bit about reading music.

- This symbol: 𝄞 is called the "Treble Clef".

- The Treble Clef is a five-line staff that is used for guitar music.

- The lines have numbers that go from 1 to 5. Line 1 is the lowest line. Line 5 is the top line (or highest line) on the Treble Clef.

- To help you remember the note names of each line, memorize the saying below. In the saying ("Every Good Bird Does Fly"). "Every" stands for "E", "Good" stands for "G", "Bird" stands for "B", "Does" stands for "D", and "Fly" stands for "F".

- See the chart below to better understand these notes.

From bottom to top, this is the pattern for the lines: E, G, B, D, F

Line Numbers

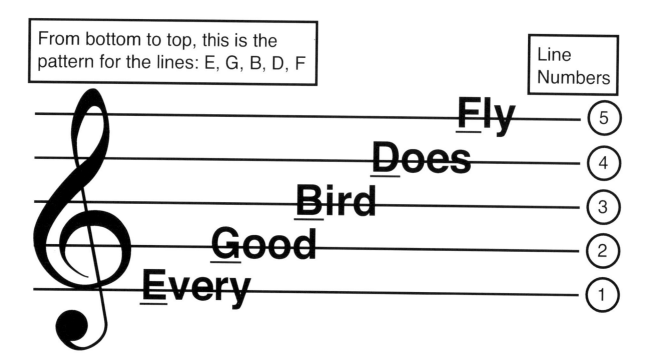

Treble Clef Game: The Lines

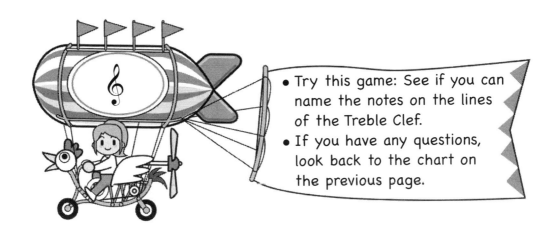

- Try this game: See if you can name the notes on the lines of the Treble Clef.
- If you have any questions, look back to the chart on the previous page.

The letter names are inside the notes for the first line. You may check back on the notes from this line if you have questions later on in the game. Have Fun!

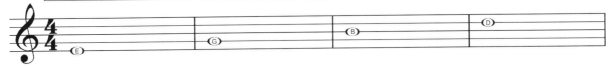

The Treble Clef Spaces: Overview

• The Treble Clef also has four spaces.

• These are the parts of the clef between the five lines.

• The spaces have numbers that go from 1 to 4. Space 1 is the lowest space. Space 4 is the top space (or highest space) on the Treble Clef.

• To help you learn the note names of each space, remember that the spaces of the Treble Clef form the word "Face" spelled upside down (from bottom space to top.)

• See the chart below to better understand these notes.

From bottom to top, this is the pattern for the Spaces: F, A, C, E

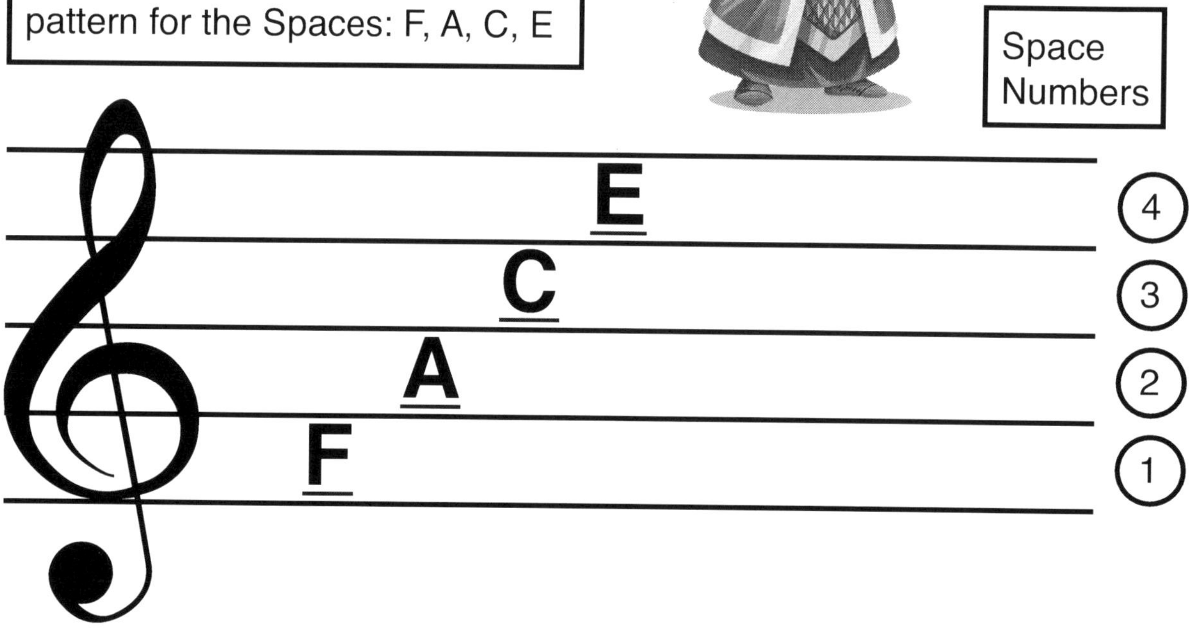

Space Numbers

Treble Clef Game: The Spaces

Let's play another game!
This time, let's name the notes for the Treble Clef spaces.
Have Fun!

The letter names are inside the notes for the first line. You may check back on the notes from this line if you have questions later on in the game. Have Fun!

Treble Clef Notes: B, C, and D

- Now, we are going to learn a little bit more about reading music.

- Remember, this symbol: is called the "Treble Clef"

- The Treble Clef is a five-line staff that is used for guitar music.
- The Treble Clef is made up of Lines and Spaces that correspond to notes on the guitar.
- We will learn more about the lines and spaces of the Treble Clef in the following lessons.

B

- **B** is on the 3rd line of the Treble Clef.

- Play **B** on the open B string.

- Take a look at the chart on the right and play **B** on your guitar's open 2nd string.

The Note B

C

This is the TrebleClef Symbol:

- **C** is on the 3rd space of the Treble Clef.

- Play **C** with your pointer finger.

- Take a look at the chart on the right and play **C** on the 1st fret of the 2nd string.

The Note C

D

- **D** is on the 4th line of the Treble Clef.

- Play **D** with your ring finger.

- Take a look at the chart on the right and play **D** on the 3rd fret of the 2nd string.

The Note D

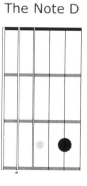

Treble Clef Song: Wizards

- Let's play this song that uses the notes C, D, and E of the Treble Clef.
- If you have any questions about the letter names, take a look back at the previous few pages in the book. *Have Fun!*

Why did the chicken cross the road?

I know that the answer is in here somewhere?

Wizards

The letter names are inside the notes for the first line. You may check back on the notes from this line if you have questions later on in the song. Have Fun!

Treble Clef Notes: E, F, and G

Let's now take a look at some of the notes on the Treble Clef that can be played on the High-E String on your guitar. That's the 1st string.

E

- **E** is on the 4th space of the Treble Clef.
- Play **E** on the open High-E string.
- Take a look at the chart on the right and play **E** on your guitar's open 1st string.

The Note E

F

This is the TrebleClef Symbol:

- **F** is on the 5th line of the Treble Clef.
- Play **F** with your pointer finger.
- Take a look at the chart on the right and play **F** on the 1st fret of the 1st string.

The Note F

G

- **G** sits on top of the Treble Clef.
- Play **G** with your ring finger.
- Take a look at the chart on the right and play **G** on the 3rd fret of the 1st string.

The Note G

Happy Dog: A Song for the Treble Clef with the Notes B, C, D, E, F, and G

In a few pages, we're going to learn "Happy Birthday"!

The letter names are inside the notes for the first line. You may check back on the notes from this line if you have questions later on in the song. Have Fun!

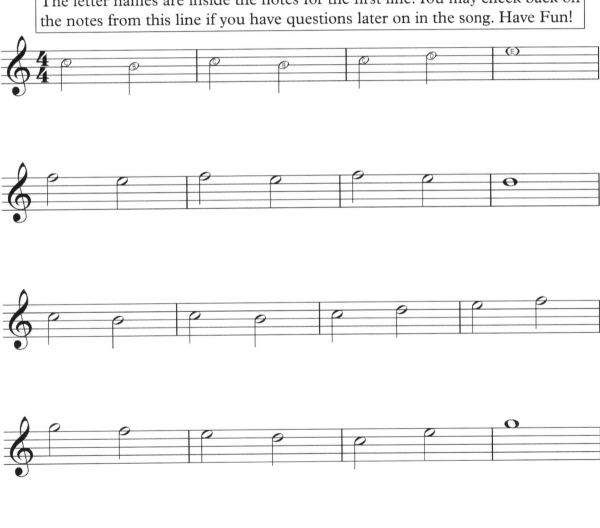

Sad Dog: A Song for the Treble Clef with the Notes B, C, D, E, F & G

The letter names are inside the notes for the first line. You may check back on the notes from this line if you have questions later on in the song. Have Fun!

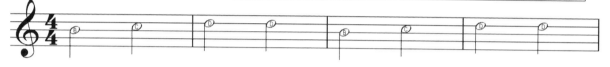

Kum-Bah-Yah: A New Note: A

- Let's add a new note A, which is on top of the Treble Clef.
- There is a line through the note A.
- For *Kum-Bah-Yah,* play the note G with your pointer finger.

A

- **A** sits above the Treble Clef.
- Play **A** with your ring finger.
- Take a look at the chart on the right and play **A** on the 5th fret of the 1st string.

The Note A

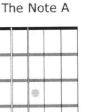

The first two notes are part of an upbeat figure. Count "1, 2, 3, 4" and start on beat 3.

Kum Bah Yah, My Lord, Kum-Bah-Yah_____ Kum-Bah- Yah, My Lord,

The note names have been added inside the notes to make playing the song a bit easier. Also remember to play the G with your pointer finger and the A with your ring finger.

Kum-Bah - Yah_____ Kum-Bah - Yah, My Lord, Kum-Bah - Yah._____

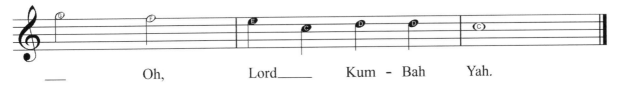

___ Oh, Lord_____ Kum - Bah Yah.

Happy Birthday

The Muffin Man

We have a new note: A. It is on the 2nd fret of the 3rd string (the G string). Take a look at the chart on the right for more information.

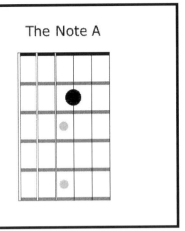

The Note A

The letter names are inside the notes for the song. Have Fun!

53

Farmer in the Dell

The letter names are inside the notes for the song. Have Fun!

Start playing on the 3rd beat here.

This little, black box is a rest for 2 beats.

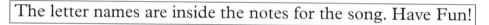

The farm - er   in   the   dell._____   The farm - er

This note (G) is the open 3rd string.

This E is tied. Hold it down for six beats.

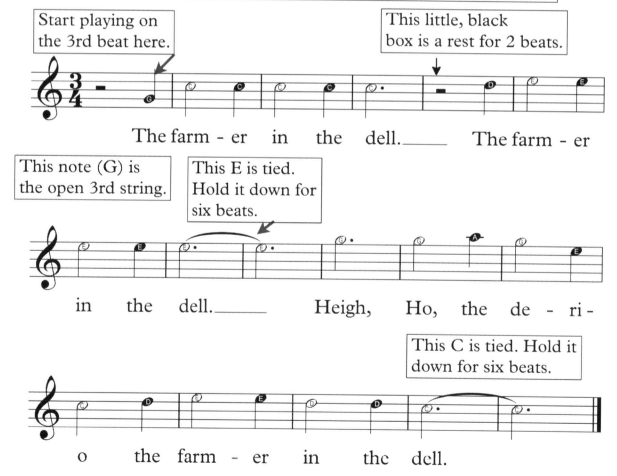

in   the   dell._____   Heigh,   Ho,   the   de - ri -

This C is tied. Hold it down for six beats.

o   the   farm - er   in   the   dell.

Hickory Dickory Dock

The letter names are inside the notes for the song. Have Fun!

| Hick | - | or | - | y | Dick | - | or | - | y |

| Dock. | The | mouse | ran |

| up | the | clock. |

| The | clock | struck |

| one | and | down | he |

| ran. | Hick | - | or | - | y |

| Dick | - | or | - | y | Dock. |

What are Eighth Notes?

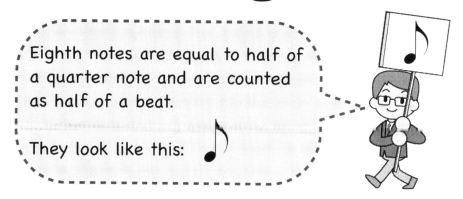

Eighth notes are equal to half of a quarter note and are counted as half of a beat.

They look like this:

In a measure of 4/4 time, eight eighth notes would be counted counted like this: 1 &, 2 &, 3 &, 4 &. The "&" stands for the word "and". The "&" or "and" is the halfway point of a beat. See the example below:

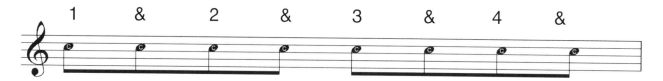

Musicians often refer to the halfway point of a beat as the "and". For example, a musician might say, "play it on the _and_ of _two_". This would mean: play it at the halfway point of beats two and three.

When you divide a beat into sections, it is called "subdividing". Let's practice counting and playing groups of eighth notes and quarter notes. Remember to subdivide the eighth notes: for example, 1 &, 2 &, 3 &, 4 &. Try these exercises on the note C (the 1st fret of the 2nd string).

Alphabet Song

The letter names are inside the notes for the song. Have Fun!

A, B, C, D, E, F, G,

These 4 notes are eighth notes. They are each equal to half a beat. Count: 1 & 2 &.

H, I, J, K, L, M, N, O, P,

Q, R, S, T, U, V,

These 2 notes are eighth notes. Count: 1 &.

W,_____ X, Y, and Z.

Now, I know my A B Cs

Next time won't you sing with me

Some New Notes: D, E & F

For *Silent Night,* we have a few new notes on the 4th string of our guitar. Take a moment to look at the three charts below and try out the notes. Feel free to look back at this page if you have any questions.

We have a new note: D. It is the open 4th string (the D string). Take a look at the chart on the right for more information.

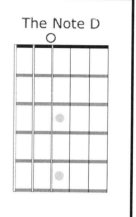

The Note D

We have a new note: E. It is on the 2nd fret of the 4th string (the D string). Take a look at the chart on the right for more information.

The Note E

We have a new note: F. It is on the 3rd fret of the 4th string (the D string). Take a look at the chart on the right for more information.

The Note F

Silent Night

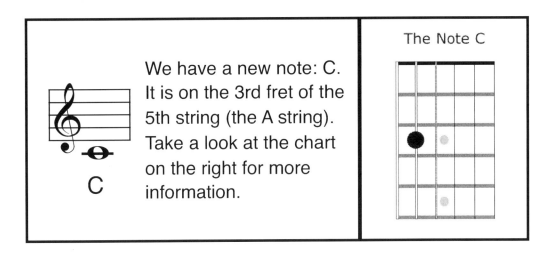

We have a new note: C. It is on the 3rd fret of the 5th string (the A string). Take a look at the chart on the right for more information.

The Note C

C

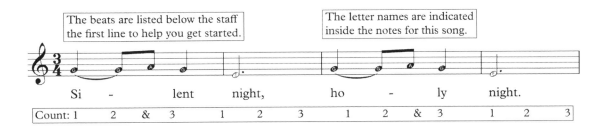

The beats are listed below the staff the first line to help you get started.

The letter names are indicated inside the notes for this song.

Si - lent night, ho - ly night.

Count: 1   2   &   3   1   2   3   1   2   &   3   1   2   3

All   is   calm.   All   is   bright.   'Round   yon

vir - gin   Moth - er and   Child.   Ho - ly   In - fant so

ten - der and   mild.   Sleep   in   heav - en - ly   peace.

Sleep_____   in   heav - en - ly   peace.

59

Row, Row, Row Your Boat

Row, row, row your boat gent - ly down the stream._____ Mer - ri - ly, mer - ri - ly, mer - ri - ly, mer - ri - ly, life is but a

dream.

Shenandoah

_____
(Song Title)

Now, try writing your own song with the notes that we have learned. Feel free to use whole notes, half notes, quarter notes, and eighth notes. Have fun and be creative!

Red River Valley

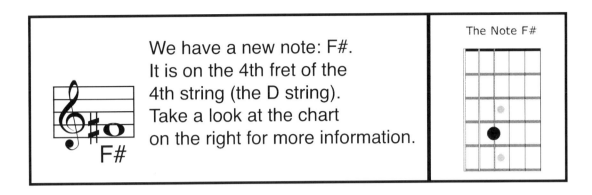

Home on the Range

Oh, give me a

home where the buf - fa - lo

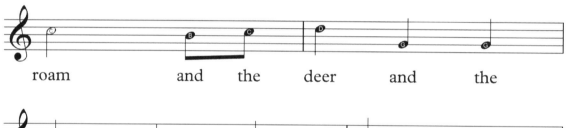

roam and the deer and the

an - ti - lope play.

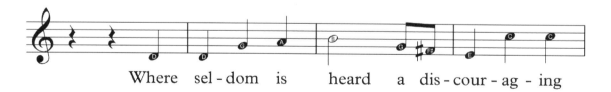

Where sel - dom is heard a dis - cour - ag - ing

word a the skys are not

cloud - y all day.

Home, home on the

range, where the deer and the

an - ti - lope play.

Where sel - dom is

heard a dis - cour - ag - ing

word and the skys are not

cloud - y all day.

This Little Light of Mine

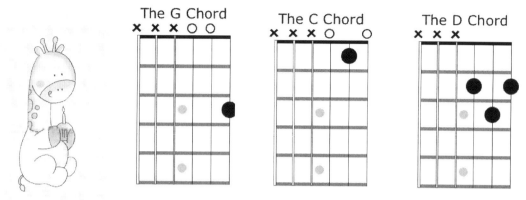

The G Chord
x x x O O

The C Chord
x x x O   O

The D Chord
x x x

- For *This Little Light of Mine,* we can choose to play the melody (the tune) or strum the chords.
- The letters for the chords are written above each measure. Strum the chords four times for each measure.
- These three chords only use the top three strings of your guitar. Take a look at the three diagrams above and try practicing the three chords.

This letter ("G") stands for the G Chord. Strum the chords 4 times for each measure.

G   G   G   G

This lit - tle light of   mine   I'm gon - na let   it   shine.

This letter ("C") stands for the C Chord.

C   C   C   G

This lit - tle light of   mine   I'm gon - na let   it   shine.

G   G   G   G

This lit - tle light of   mine   I'm gon-na let   it   shine.   Let   it

This letter ("D") stands for the D Chord.

G   D   G

shine.   Let   it   shine.   Let   it   shine.

Simple Gifts

68

Lullaby

Strum each chord 3
times for each measure.

Johannes Brahms

69

New

Bonus

Lessons!

For this new edition, we have added some free, bonus lessons and songs in the following pages.

There are a few new techniques, like reading tablature and alternate picking.

We hope that you enjoy these bonus lessons!

Have fun!!

Tablature Basics

Guitar tablature (or TAB for short) is a notation system that graphically indicates guitar fingering, rather than the actual notes and pitches to be played. In other words, TAB shows you the exact location on strings and frets where you will need to play, but it does <u>not</u> tell you the actual notes (for example, "Eb", G, B) or the rhythms and durations of what you will be playing. Tablature is a good initial "shorthand" notation, especially if you are already familiar with a song, but it might have some drawbacks if you solely rely on it to learn music. For this book, we will use tablature and video examples. Later on in your playing, you might like to start learning standard notation, which will give you a more accurate representation of what's going on in music than tablature.

Here is how TAB works: The thickest string (Low-E string) is the bottom line of the tablature staff and the thinnest string (High-E string) is the top line of the tablature staff. So, the higher lines on the staff represent the higher-pitched guitar strings and the lower lines on the tablature staff represent the lower-pitched guitar strings. A note on the guitar is indicated by placing a number on one of the lines of the tablature staff. The number represents which fret to place your finger on and the line indicates which string to play. However, tablature does <u>not</u> indicate how long to play the note, which left-hand finger to use, or how loud to play the note. As mentioned above, it does <u>not</u> indicate the actual name of the note ("pitch") that you are playing. It does, though, sometimes indicate other qualities of the note--for example, if you are supposed to bend the note, play a pull off or hammer on, or give vibrato (more about all of these techniques later on in the book).

Chords are represented by placing the numbers on top of each other on the TAB staff. The number zero indicates that you should play an open string.

Tablature Example of the C Major Chord from Lesson 10
(See the Chord chart on Lesson 10)

──────0────────	High-E String (1st String)
──────1────────	B String (2nd String)
──────0────────	G String (3rd String)
───────────────	D String (4th String)
───────────────	A String (5th String)
───────────────	Low-E String (6th String)

Aura Lee

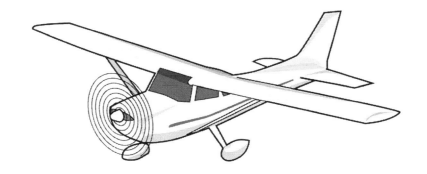

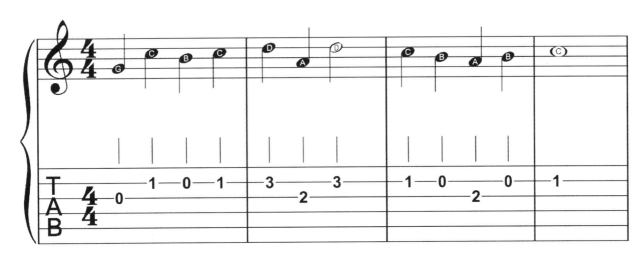

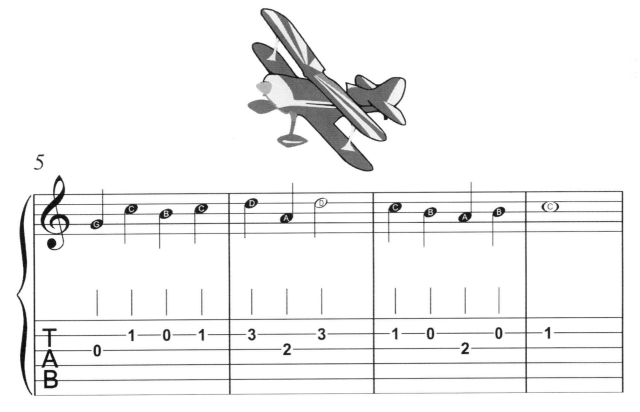

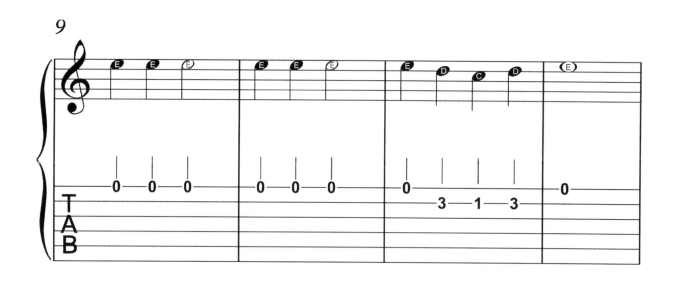

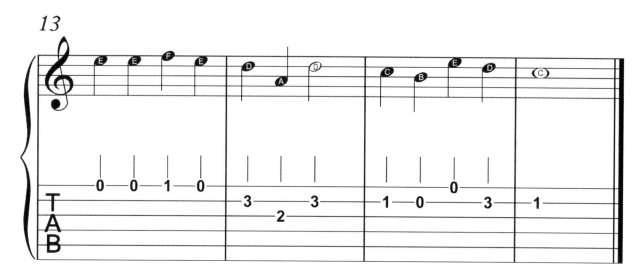

74

Bath Time!

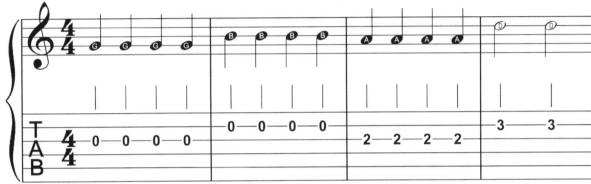

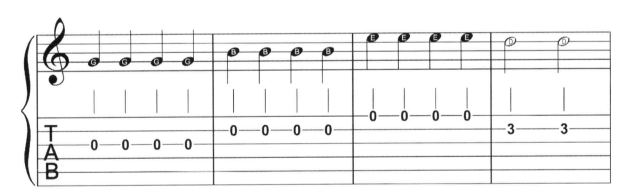

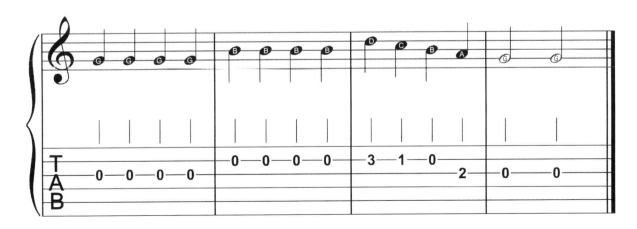

Pirate's Helper

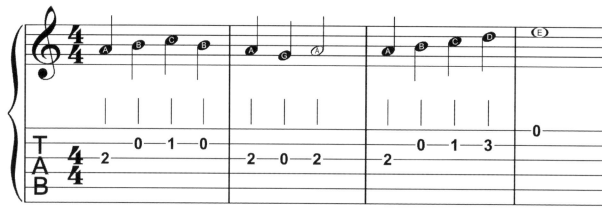

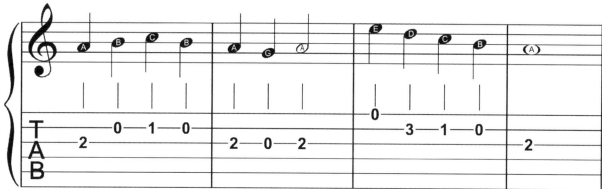

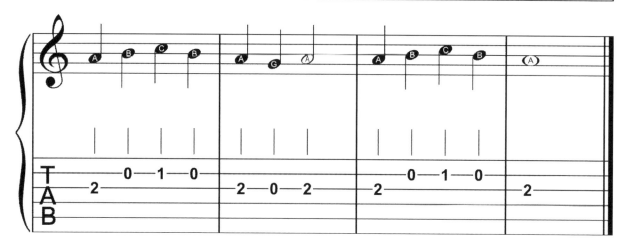

Elephant Smiles

Happy Snowman

Sleeping Bear

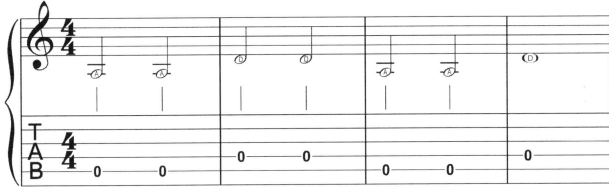

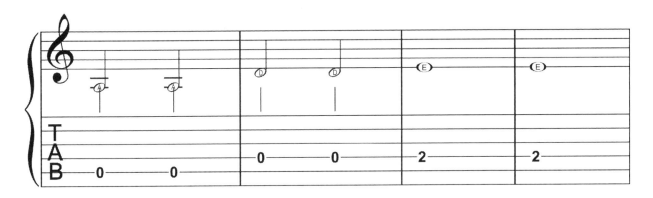

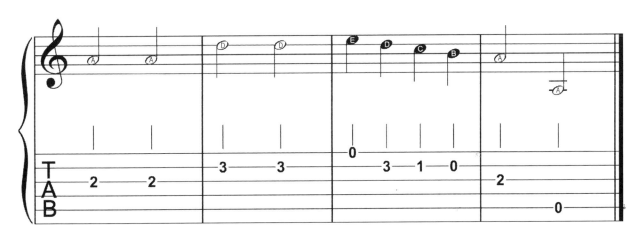

Happy Parrot

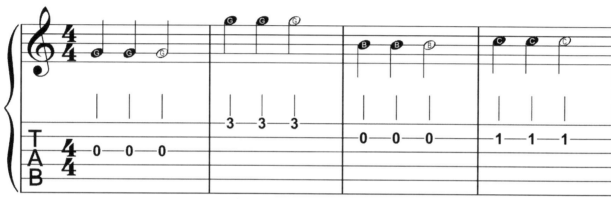

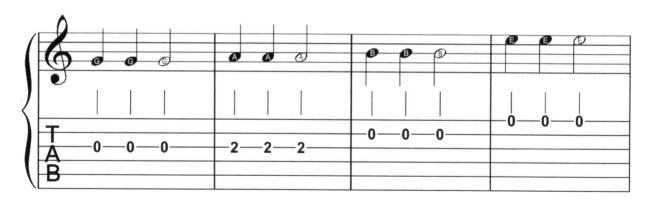

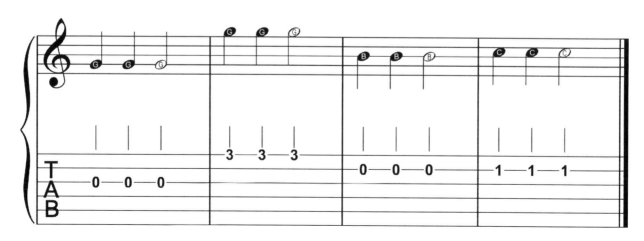

The Artistic Rabbit

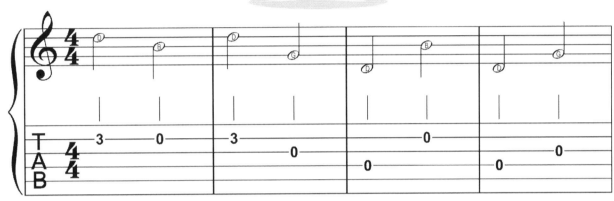

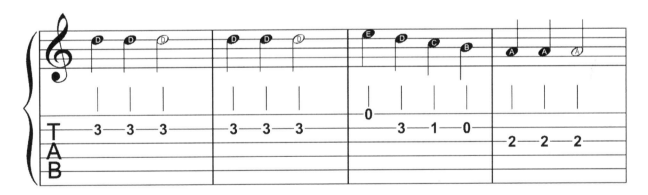

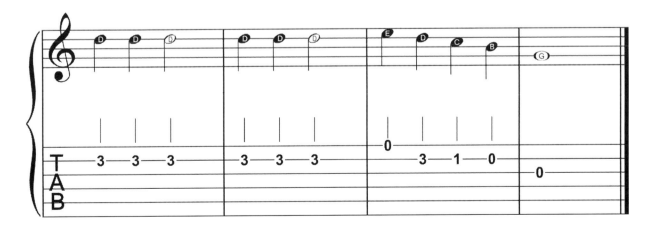

Sea Dragon

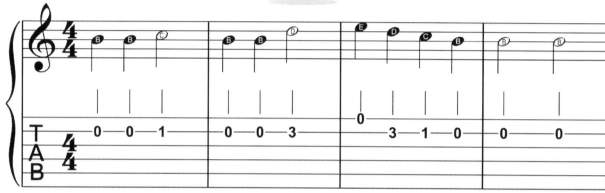

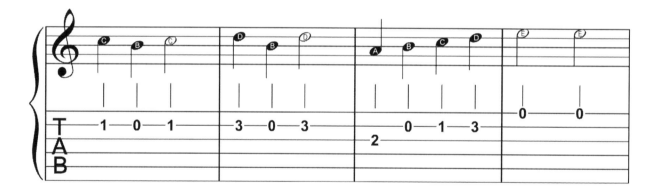

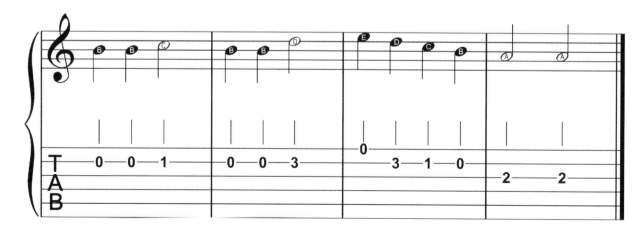

The Kangaroo

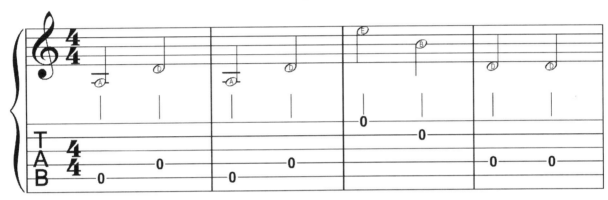

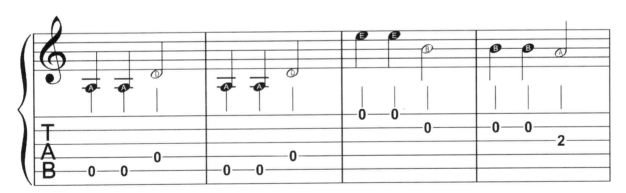

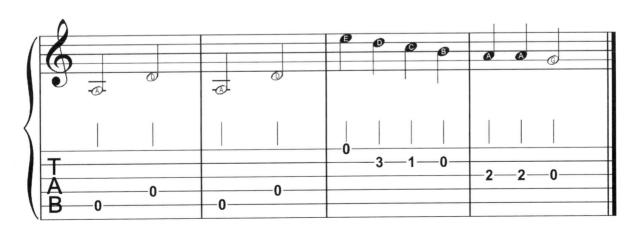

Happy Panda

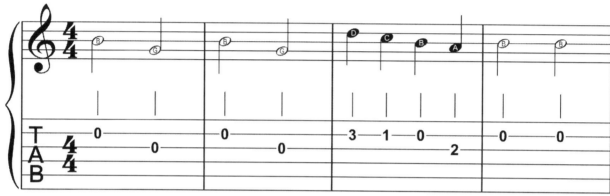

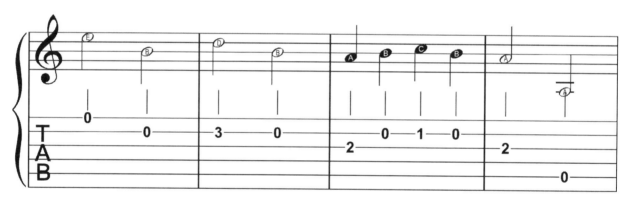

84

The Zebra

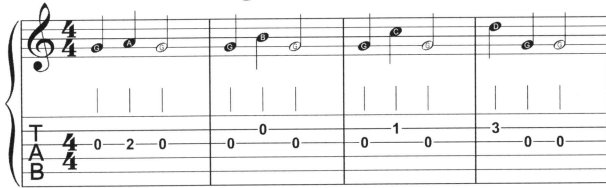

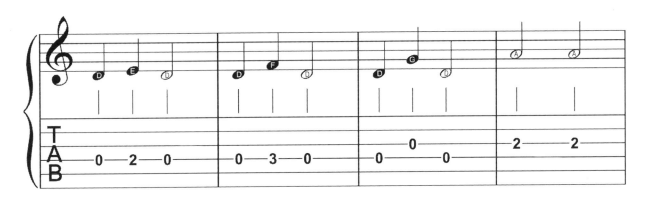

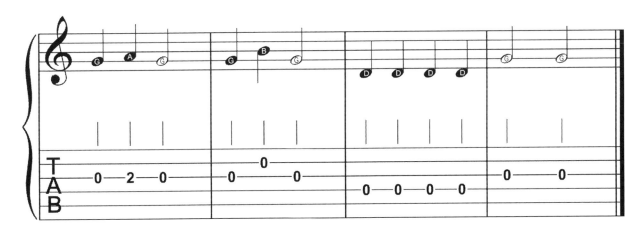

85

The Penguin

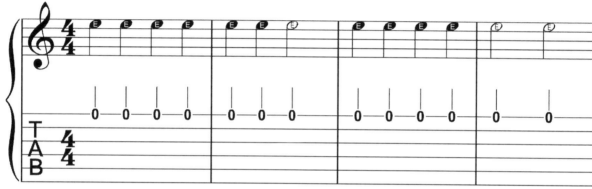

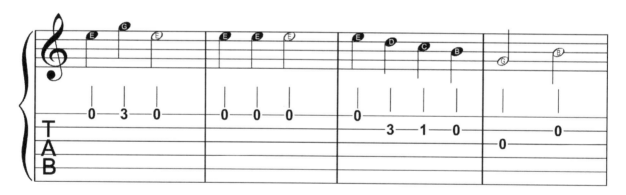

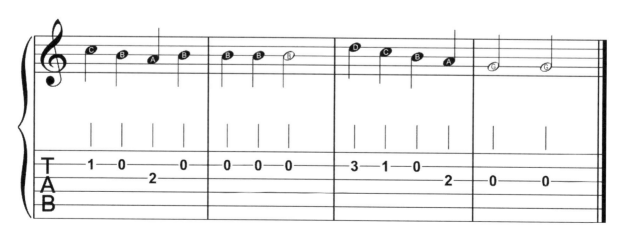

Some New Chords

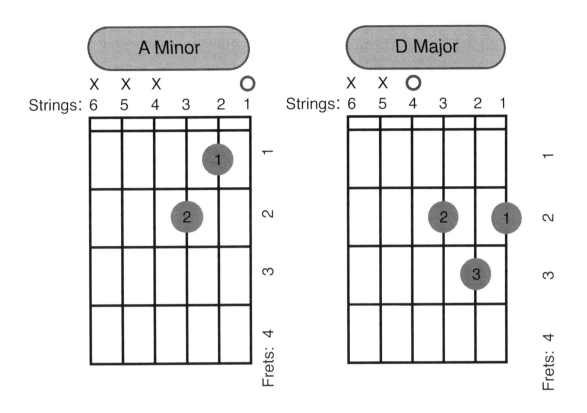

House of the Rising Sun:

For *House of the Rising Sun,* strum each chord three times. Also, if you need some help remembering the fingering for the chords, feel free to turn back to the earlier lessons in this book that go over those chords. Have fun!

House of the Rising Sun

Chord:	Am	C	D	F
	There is a	house in	New Or-	leans they
Strum:	1 2 3	1 2 3	1 2 3	1 2 3

Chord:	Am	C	E	E
	call the	ris- ing	sun.	It's
Strum:	1 2 3	1 2 3	1 2 3	1 2 3

Chord:	Am	C	D	F
	been the	ruin of	many poor	souls and
Strum:	1 2 3	1 2 3	1 2 3	1 2 3

Chord:	Am	E	Am	Am
	Lord, I	know I'm	one.	
Strum:	1 2 3	1 2 3	1 2 3	1 2 3

The Melody for House of the Rising Sun

In this lesson, we are going to look at the melody for *House of the Rising Sun.* The melody, in this version, sits on the middle and lower strings. There are also a number of notes on the open strings of the guitar.

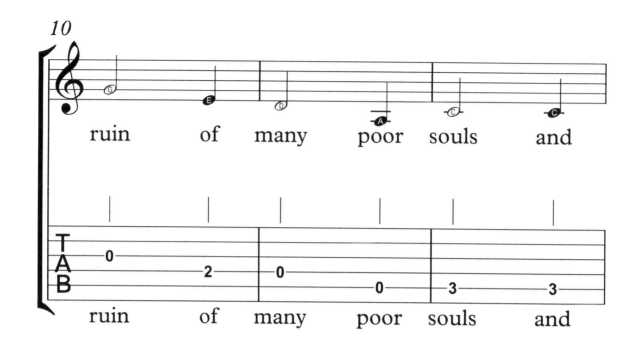

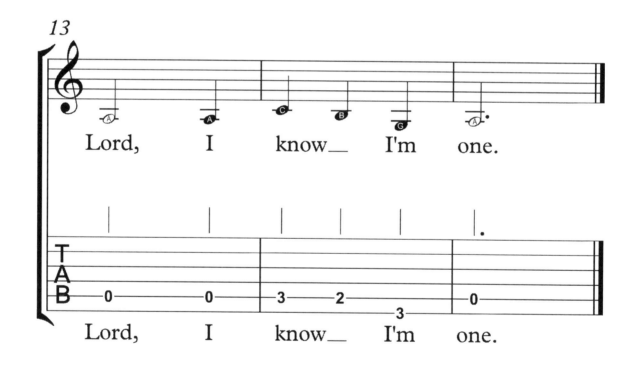

Alternate Picking

Alternate picking is a technique where the guitarist "alternates" between playing notes with downstrokes and upstrokes of the pick. This allows for much more efficient picking than just moving the pick in one direction, for example, only picking down or only picking up. (For more information on alternate picking and other guitar techniques, you might want to check out *Guitar Scales Handbook*).

Here are two alternate-picking exercises (in tablature / TAB format) to improve your right-hand picking technique. Repeat each exercise at a comfortable tempo for between 1 and 2 minutes. If your hands start to feel tired, just shake them out and take a break for a while.

⊓ : This symbol stands for a downstroke.

∨ : This symbol stands for an upstroke.

⊓ ∨ ⊓ ∨ ⊓ ∨ ⊓ ∨

0 1 0 1 0 1 0 1 — High-E String (1st String)
— B String (2nd String)
— G String (3rd String)
— D String (4th String)
— A String (5th String)
— Low-E String (6th String)

⊓ ∨ ⊓ ∨ ⊓ ∨ ⊓ ∨

1 2 1 2 1 2 1 2 — High-E String (1st String)
— B String (2nd String)
— G String (3rd String)
— D String (4th String)
— A String (5th String)
— Low-E String (6th String)

Minor Chords & Scarborough Fair

Here are two new chords and the famous song *Scarborough Fair.* The song is in 3/4 time; so count "1, 2, 3" for each measure.

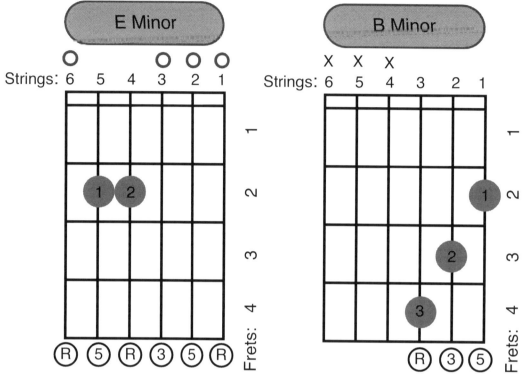

Scarborough Fair

Chord:	**Em**	**G**	**D**	**Em**	**Em**
	Are you	going to	Scarborough	Fair?	
Strum:	1 2 3	1 2 3	1 2 3	1 2 3	1 2 3

Chord:	**G**	**Em**	**A**	**Em**	**Em**
	Parsley	Sage Rose-	mary and	thyme	Oh,
Strum:	1 2 3	1 2 3	1 2 3	1 2 3	1 2 3

Chord:	**Em**	**G**	**C**	**D**	**D**
	send my	love to	one who lives	there.	For
Strum:	1 2 3	1 2 3	1 2 3	1 2 3	1 2 3

Chord:	**Em**	**D**	**C**	**Em**	**Em**
	she once	was a	true love of	mine.	
Strum:	1 2 3	1 2 3	1 2 3	1 2 3	1 2 3

The Melody for Scarborough Fair

Here is the melody for *Scarborough Fair*. It utilizes open strings and spans the middle to the upper strings of the guitar. Take your time to practice each line of music before putting it all together.

Are you go - ing to Scar - bo - rough Fair?

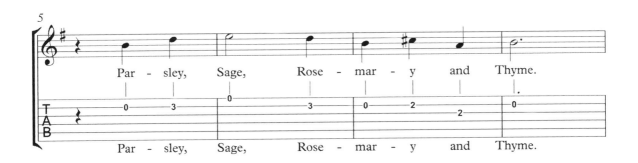

Par - sley, Sage, Rose - mar - y and Thyme.

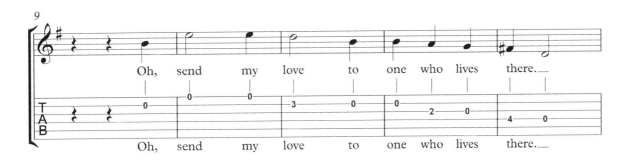

Oh, send my love to one who lives there. __

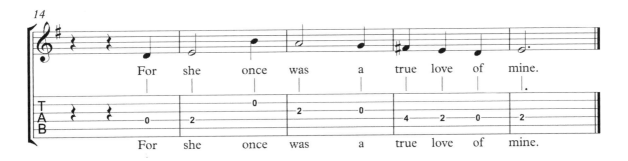

For she once was a true love of mine.

Greensleeves

Verse Section ⬭ *Greensleeves*

Chord:	**Am**	**Am**	**G**	**G**	**Am**
	A-las my	love, you	do me	wrong to	cast me
Strum:	1 2 3	1 2 3	1 2 3	1 2 3	1 2 3
Chord:	**Am**	**E**	**E**	**Am**	**Am**
	off dis-	courteous-	ly when	I have	loved
Strum:	1 2 3	1 2 3	1 2 3	1 2 3	1 2 3
Chord:	**G**	**G**	**Am**	**E**	**Am**
	you so	long, de-	light- ing	in your	com-pan-
Strum:	1 2 3	1 2 3	1 2 3	1 2 3	1 2 3

Chord:	**Am**
	y
Strum:	1 2 3

Chorus Section (Go to the Next Line)

Chord:	**C**	**C**	**G**	**G**
	Green	Sleeves was	all my	joy and
Strum:	1 2 3	1 2 3	1 2 3	1 2 3
Chord:	**Am**	**Am**	**E**	**E**
	Green	Sleeves was	my de-	light.
Strum:	1 2 3	1 2 3	1 2 3	1 2 3
Chord:	**C**	**C**	**G**	**G**
	Green	Sleeves was	heart of	gold and
Strum:	1 2 3	1 2 3	1 2 3	1 2 3
Chord:	**Am**	**E**	**Am**	**Am**
	who but my	lady	Green	Sleeves.
Strum:	1 2 3	1 2 3	1 2 3	1 2 3

The Melody for Greensleeves (Chorus Section)

> This is the melody for the chorus section of *Greensleeves.* Most of the notes sit on the top three strings of the guitar: High-E, B, and G.

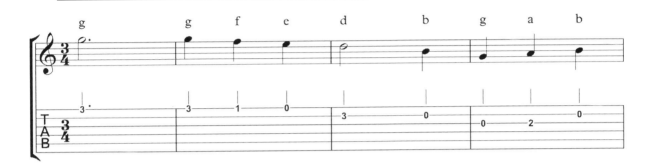

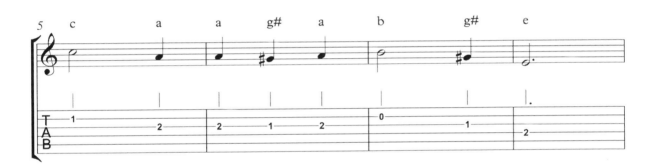

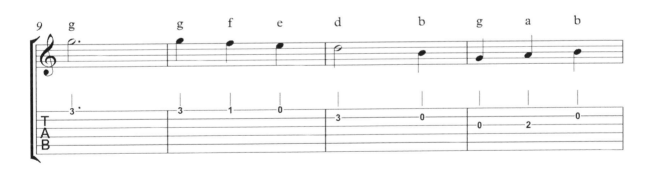

Surprise Symphony Theme

Here is a famous theme from the great composer Joseph Haydn!

Joseph Haydn

Joy to the World

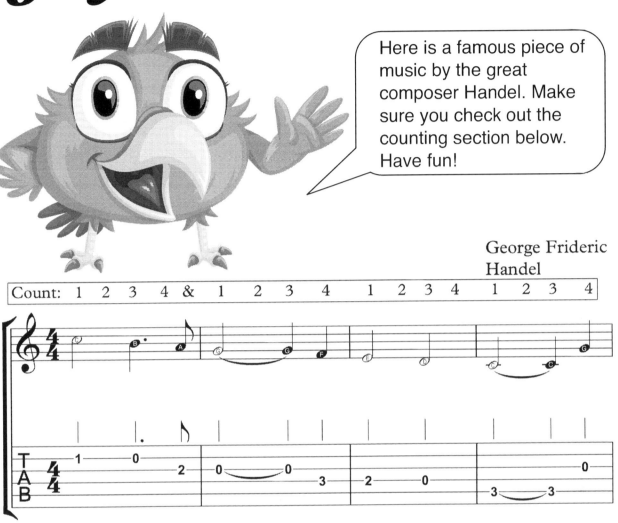

George Frideric Handel

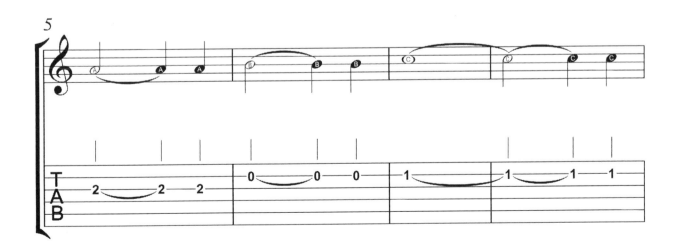

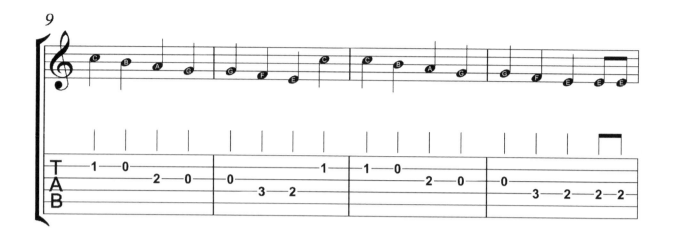

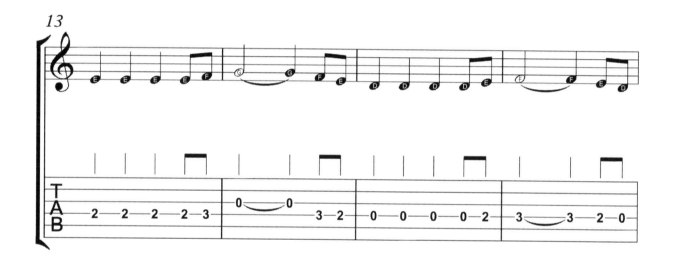

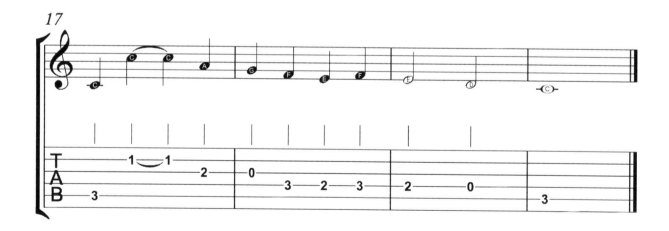

Pachelbel Canon

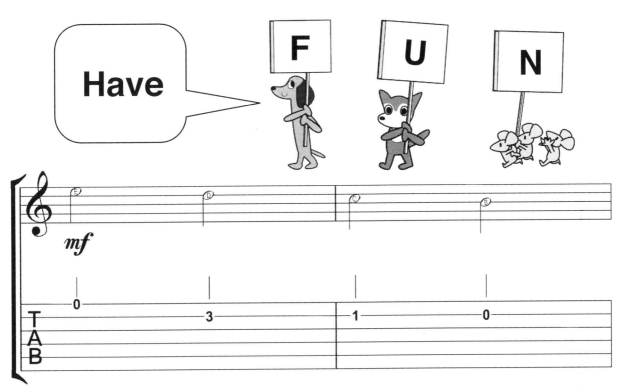

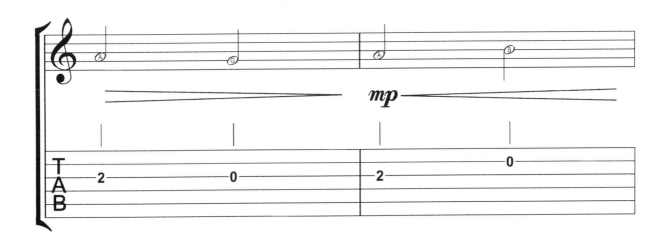

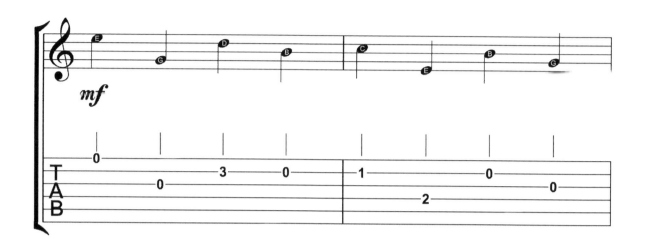

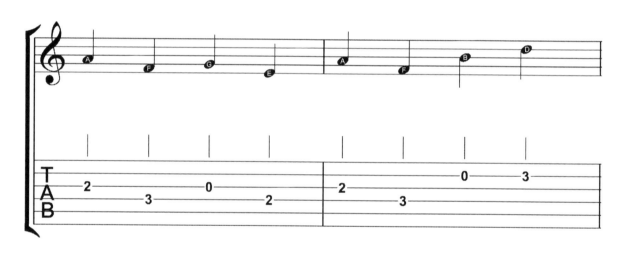

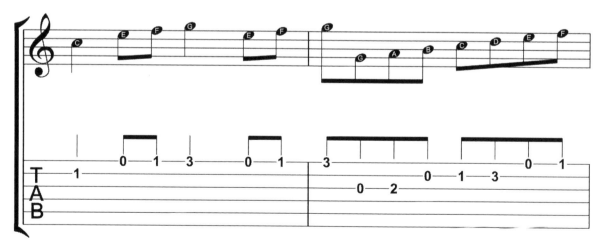

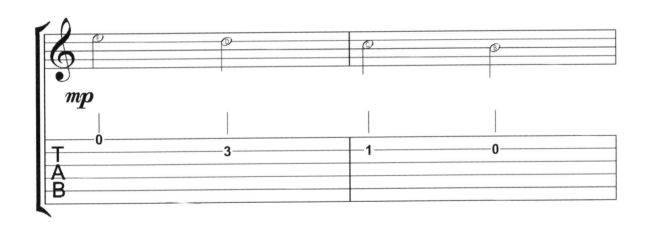

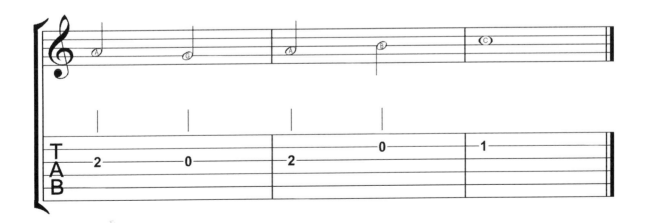

Congratulations!
You have completed the Book!

Great work in completing this book and video course on the basics of guitar. You now have an understanding of the fundamentals of guitar playing: basic guitar technique, beginner-level note reading and chord playing, a repertoire of songs and pieces to perform for family and friends, and some understanding of music fundamentals--such as time signatures, beats, and the staff.

To continue to the next level, I would suggest this book and video course:

• *Guitar Book for Kids Songbook* (Available in December 2019)

Keep up the good work and continue to practice and play the guitar!

Damon Ferrante

If you enjoyed this book, please recommend the paperback edition to your local library.

Damon Ferrante is a composer, guitarist, and professor of piano studies. He has taught on the music faculties of Seton Hall University and Montclair State University. For over 20 years, Damon has taught guitar, piano, composition, and music theory. Damon has had performances at Carnegie Hall, Symphony Space, and throughout the US and Europe. His main teachers have been David Rakowski at Columbia University, Stanley Wolfe at Juilliard, and Bruno Amato at the Peabody Conservatory of Johns Hopkins University. Damon has written two operas, a guitar concerto, song cycles, orchestral music, and numerous solo and chamber music works. He has over 30 music books and scores in print. For more information on his books, concerts, and music, please visit steeplechasearts.com.

CERTIFICATE
of ACCOMPLISHMENT

This certifies that

_____
(sign your name)

Has successfully completed the training
program requirement for

Guitar Book for Kids

and is ready to begin

Guitar for Kids Songbook

DATE   TEACHER

GREAT JOB!

Lesson Checklist: Page 1

Use this Checklist to Keep Track of Your Progress:

Page #	Completed / Check	Date

Lesson Checklist: Page 2

Use this Checklist to Keep Track of Your Progress:

Page #	Completed / Check	Date

Lesson Checklist:
Page 3

Use this Checklist to Keep Track of Your Progress:

Page #	Completed / Check	Date

Lesson Checklist: Page 4

Use this Checklist to Keep Track of Your Progress:

Page #	Completed / Check	Date

Lesson Checklist: Page 5

Use this Checklist to Keep Track of Your Progress:

Page #	Completed / Check	Date

You might also Enjoy these books by Damon Ferrante

Little Piano Book
for Children 5 & Up

No Music Reading Required

Damon Ferrante

Fun, Easy, Step-By-Step, Teach-Yourself Song and Beginner Piano Guide
Book & Streaming Videos

Available in December 2019

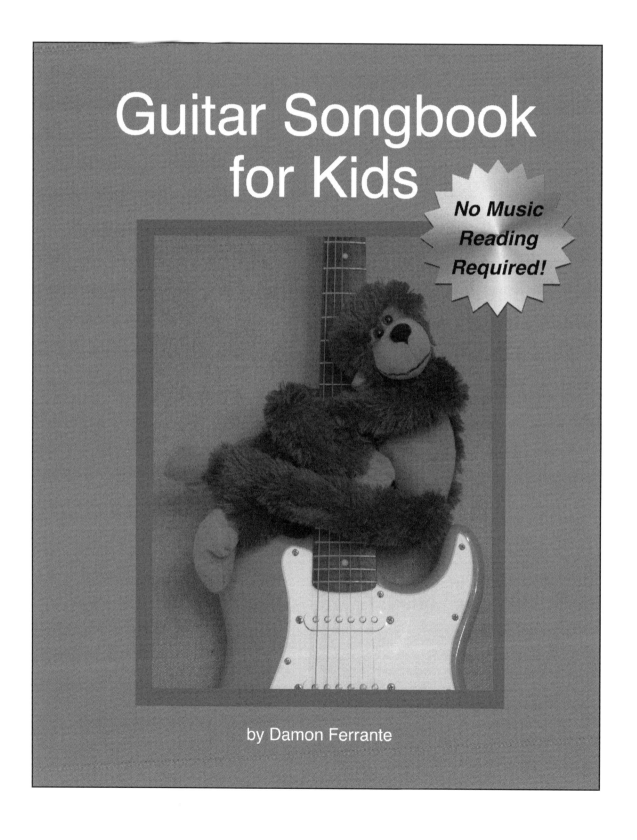

Guitar Songbook for Kids

No Music Reading Required!

by Damon Ferrante

Beginner Rock Guitar Lessons

Guitar Instruction Guide to Learn How to Play Licks, Chords, Scales, Techniques, Lead & Rhythm Guitar - Teach Yourself

No Music Reading Required!

Damon Ferrante

Book, Streaming Videos & TAB

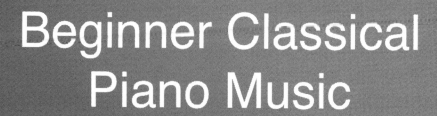

Beginner Classical Piano Music

Teach Yourself How to Play Famous Piano Pieces by Bach, Mozart, Beethoven & the Great Composers

Includes Streaming Videos!

Damon Ferrante

Book, Streaming Videos & MP3 Audio

Piano Book for Adult Beginners

Teach Yourself How to Play Famous Piano Songs, Read Music, Theory & Technique

No Music Reading Required!

Damon Ferrante

Book & Streaming Video Lessons

We want to help you become the guitarist of your dreams!

Check Out Steeplechasemusic.com for Free Guitar Lessons in Your Inbox!

Made in the USA
Monee, IL
27 September 2020